ALSO BY LEWIS WARSH

POETRY
The Suicide Rates
Highjacking
Moving Through Air
Chicago, with Tom Clark
Dreaming As One
Long Distance
Immediate Surrounding
Today
Blue Heaven
Hives
Methods of Birth Control
The Corset
Information from the Surface of Venus
Avenue of Escape
Private Agenda, with Pamela Lawton
The Origin of the World
Debtor's Prison, with Julie Harrison
Reported Missing
Flight Test
The Flea Market in Kiel
Inseparable: Poems 1995-2005

FICTION
Agnes & Sally
A Free Man
Money Under the Table
Ted's Favorite Skirt
A Place in the Sun
One Foot Out the Door: Collected Stories

AUTOBIOGRAPHY
Part of My History
The Maharajah's Son
Bustin's Island, 1968

EDITOR
The Angel Hair Anthology, with Anne Waldman

RECORDING
The Origin of the World

TRANSLATION
Night of Loveless Nights by Robert Desnos

ALIEN ABDUCTION

ISBN 978-1-937027-43-8
First Edition, First Printing, 2015

Ugly Duckling Presse
The Old American Can Factory
232 Third St., E-303, Brooklyn, NY 11215
uglyducklingpresse.org

Distributed in the USA by SPD / Small Press Distribution
Distributed in Canada via Coach House Books by Raincoast Books
Distributed in the UK by Inpress Books

Cover art by Max Warsh
Design by Doormouse
Typeset in Bembo and Avenir Next

Printed and bound by McNaughton & Gunn, Saline, MI
Covers printed letterpress at UDP on paper from French Paper Company, Niles, MI

Funding for this book was provided by generous grants from the National Endowment
for the Arts, the Department of Cultural Affairs for New York City, and the New York
State Council on the Arts.

ALIEN ABDUCTION

LEWIS WARSH

Ugly Duckling Presse
Brooklyn, NY

CONTENTS

for

Marie, Sophia,
Max, Alyssa,
Zola and Katt

SUPERFICIAL THINGS

Rousseau said something about something.
He said something.
He said: I'm going to give you a fat lip.

The doorman held the umbrella
over the head of the woman
with the poodle. She was taking
her dog to the vet.
The doorman walked out into the middle
of the street and called a taxi.
He put his arm in the air but the taxis
wouldn't stop. One of the taxis
splashed water from a puddle onto
his uniform.

It was like a scene in the movie
The Birds when the actress played
by Tippi Hedren runs down a road followed
by the birds pecking at her skin.
But maybe I'm thinking of Suzanne
Pleshette instead? Wasn't she the
actress who got pecked to death
by the birds? Not Suzanne Pleshette,
but the character in the movie.

Lack of sleep is no excuse
for stupidity. I can only retrace
my steps down the side of
the mountain once too often.
I tried to climb the hill but my
feet were caught in the mud

and the dogs were barking
around a distant bonfire.

The Vietnam War happened. In those
days there was a draft. A letter
arrived and you had to show up
somewhere downtown and take a physical.
I went armed with a letter from my
eye doctor saying my eyes didn't work
together. It's true, it was all true,
but they ignored the letter, so I asked
to see the psychiatrist and I told him something
that wasn't true. He said: would you take
a lie detector test? I said yes.
And that was that.

She stepped out of a B-movie
and jumped into the water. Some helicopters
hover in the sky but they never
recover the body. I think I'll go down
to the drugstore and fill a prescription.
The medicine is beginning to take effect.

It was easy to win the war
as long as everyone died. And some
return home empty-handed,
armless, clueless. The apostrophe
follows the "s" for the possessive
but for the plural it comes before,
the apostrophe (in case you
didn't know) comes before the "s."

Let's begin this symphony again.
Only people with a lot of money
can afford these concerts.
Even sitting in the last row
of the top balcony is too expensive.
The men toss their hats onto the stage,
but I have to squint to see anything.

The people waiting
on line are not
the same people
who are leaving.
You can close
your windows or
wear earplugs when
you get into bed.
Hurricane John is coming,
we better tape up
the glass. Better hide
under the covers until
the storm passes
over.

Accidents happen, mainly in the home,
so you better pay attention. Like
when you slice an apple if you think
about something else at the same time
you're likely to cut off one of your fingers,
so be careful.

I hitchhiked north and spent a few nights
on the beach in Mendocino. I crawled into

my sleeping bag and stared at the stars.
I had the feeling like I was in prison, I mean
I was never so free as at that moment but I
was also locked up in a person who
wasn't "me," which might be too complicated
to explain without backpedalling a million
pages into the distant past. I mean the
motivation is always there, under the surface,
like a pact with the bad angel and the good devil
at the same time, and who knows who might
appear when you least expect it, looking down
at you from a corner of the ceiling
in broad daylight.

One sentence is ending, another beginning.
The first word of each sentence begins
with a capital letter. The last word is followed
by a period. No I mean a death sentence, something
that never ends, time warped *ad infinitum*
motes of dust in the sun.

NOCTURNE

It's possible you can see someone from
A distance, after all these years, and stop in your
Tracks or do a double take and wonder if maybe
It's just someone who looks like someone
You used to know or if it's the real person and
Then you walk on by like in the song "Walk
On By" and then you turn turn again but the person's
Gone and all you can do is haul yourself
Up to the roof and jump off or shoot yourself
In the foot so that you can't walk can't move
And time hangs heavy as you sit in your room
And wonder if that person was him or you
Or someone's twin who arrived from another
Planet to savor the lilac scent that radiates
From your skin

And the heat comes up from the pipes like *Les
Trois Gymnopédies* by Erik Satie and I turn the key
Without biting my tongue and the heart comes
Back on until it bleeds and I take back with one
Hand what I gave with the other and someone
Comes in off the street no longer invisible
And the kissing booth closes for the night—too
Bad for you—and I display my dishrag abs to
The wind one last time, feel my skin on fire
As I descend

THE MILK WAS SOUR

The milk was sour, but I drank it anyway

You must check the expiration date on the container before you buy it

I spilled the container of sour milk into the sink

The strawberries are moldy, I only bought them yesterday

It's pointless to ruin your life over love for another person

You can always go back to the store and get a refund

I ran out into the rain and went to the store for a container of milk

It's not necessary to wear clothing when you go to the store

No one in the store notices whether you're wearing clothing or not

For some animals the ritual pattern of courtship is a dance of death

Wet streets, the entrance to the bridge, the windows of stores selling
   diamonds

Go back to where you started and repeat everything you said

Once I stood where Mao stood and stared down at Tiananmen Square

And once the wind blew me backwards off the Great Wall

DEAR COMMUNARD

The satisfaction of human needs creates new needs
Marx said, just as a poem gives birth to another
Almost immediately after you finish the one before,
So there's no sense of completion and only an occasional
Word crossed out, deleted, "no completion" seems
To be the order of the day.

Something left out calls for its other,
A warm bed is all one needs, and the new poem is calling
But the operator is asleep, and the words are lost
And found again, that's the other theme—the ghosts
Of the past enter stage center, the animals and the street
People line up on the boardwalk, the ocean looms,
Scatterbrained birds of a feather fly south for the winter,
The deletions add up—the Hotel De Ville burns to the ground—
One wing of the Louvre is gone—a mural by Delacroix turns to
       ash—
The poem needs some sustenance but no one can
Give enough, that's what I was like when I was younger,
Insatiable, in my own way, so that people thought me strange
For wanting more than I had, but the mystery is in the words
"Never enough"—I might have worn them on my sleeve—
So what do you say we get down on our knees and pray
For some god of forgiveness to man the barricades?
Or do we take it as it is, as it goes, while remaining cognizant
Of what happened down through time,
All the thens and theres mingling with all the I's and yous
Until a direct address is delivered to all of Paris
On the day 100,000 Prussians did a victory lap
Down Les Champs-Élysées—and it all really happened,

Dear Communard.

DISASTER RELIEF

Disaster relief is always late
in coming, and when it arrives
no one knows what to do
first.

Building a tent in your backyard
while they rebuild the house
might be one way of claiming
your place when it no longer
exists,

saving face
when you've sold your heart
to the first person
who says "yes."

THE SONGBOOK

Once I played Pygmalion
to the Queen of Hearts. A spoon

bent out of shape,
but no matching socks.

★

Voting turnout light in local precincts.
The Incredible Shrinking Man,
War of the Worlds, The Day the Earth
Stood Still, The Blob. Point the way and I'll go.
Single me out and I'll follow.

★

A mother
reprimands a child
on a swing

The names of seasons, animals
a knock on the door

the boat
no longer seaworthy
lost at sea
with no one aboard.

★

I bend down

to tie my laces
near a fire hydrant
like a dog.

The day begins
with light
and ends
in darkness.

But I
am not awake
and you
are only a dream.

Oh who are you
who comes
out of nowhere
and remembers my name.

*

A door in the wall
that no one saw before
suddenly opened
onto a garden
where men and women
carrying parasols
sipped coffee through broken straws
and it looked like all the colors of the rainbow
had attached themselves to the undergrowth
and the shrubbery
was lit
from behind
by invisible balls

★

The coat of many colors was draped
over a chair. Yellow cabs parked in the rain

outside the mosque.

★

The morning was
like any morning,

the bridge sagging
under the weight
of moving vans

driven by movers
with trusses

the sky peppered
with its first coat
of spackle

a barge circling
below, a delicate
brushstroke,
just a tendon

★

All the acorns
have fallen in one place.

You can gather them in your
apron and scatter them on the road

An avenue of moonlight
among the ivy shirttails.

★

I thought I would
live an orderly life but
instead I made a mess
for which I have to
admit I'm not contrite
so don't even start

★

The opposite is true
The opposite might always be true
People say something and then a minute later
something else
The clouds are barely moving but when you look
at them again they're gone
Words are like shadows covering the truth
I said that it might be true, that it rings true, that
it didn't sound true
Trees are alive but inhuman, often we stand
in their shadows
Even dead things cast shadows, stones or mountains
I said something that might be true

A state of non-being

★

Dogs began barking
to frighten the strangers
who rubbed their thighs
on the ivory statues of sailors
while women who looked like sirens
spread their pinafores over mounds of granite
and punched the air with their fists,
exposing their orifices
to bewildered drivers

★

You had your chance
to say something
but the moment passes

a face you
can remember,
with no details

stayed in bed
all day
reading *Gone
With the Wind*

another version
of happiness
between piss and shit

ACROSS THE BORDER

*I keep thinking I know something about people but then
someone does something to surprise me. Someone
who I thought I knew well acts in a way I never thought
imaginable. I'd like to act out of character for once
in my life, go against my instincts, redefine myself by
expanding the border around this person I think of as
"me." There are lines I won't cross, but what if I do? A
red light goes off, a danger signal, I lose my nerve.
I'm frightened of living with the consequences of what
I do but I hate the feeling of self-importance that makes
me think I have the power to hurt anyone. The only
person you ever end up hurting is yourself. I need
someone to take my hand and help me cross the line.*

*

*Today we went early to our favorite restaurant,
La Fonda, drank beer and ate enchiladas. The person
at the next table was eating what looked like
the head of a fish, but it might have been a human
head, for all I know. The waiter, Ernesto, brought us
our food in record time. The outdoor garden was
crowded with American couples and Mexican families.
It was New Year's Eve and the restaurant was closing
early. The sailboat on the horizon is still there.
The Malecón is almost empty. The ferry to Mazatlan
is waiting to leave, an 18 hour ride across the Sea
of Cortez. I'd like to see Mazatlan, but not tonight.*

DARK SIDE OF TIME

Time is the solution in which the living
and the dead confer—there's no other place for us
or them and there's no other place to be
(except where we are), putting our feet up
on the balcony and staring out at the empty
plain—where everything is invisible and everyone
has a name (the only way back is the way
you came), and once I played Odysseus
to her Penelope, way back when, and we stepped
from the bath in someone else's house,
and once all the lights went out in the middle
of the night and we built a fire until the storm
abated, and later—it's getting late in the day—
we'll have caviar and champagne—at the edge
of the crater on the Sea of Dreams,
and look down to earth as if it was all one
and the same, and leave our footprints
for those who follow.

THE FACTS

The facts seem to be hidden under a rock.
The truth is the pinhead of light at the window.
The facts can only reflect the truth.
It's like walking into a room
where people are sleeping on top
of the sheets, the heat coming up
through the pipes for the first time.

Nothing adds up, guilt or innocence. The
jury was deadlocked, we can all go home.
The witnesses were too intimidated to tell
the truth when they took the stand.
Nothing is true for more than a moment.
If it was up to me, I'd stay in bed
until noon.

The train leaves at 11:30. The train leaves
on track 9. Crane your neck so you can see
the numbers on the big board. You can say
that it's a fact: the train is leaving and now
I'm gone, even though outer facts often contradict
inner truth. It's more than I can handle
to put the pieces together, without losing
my balance and falling into the icy crevasse.

STANDING ROOM ONLY

More years than I can tell have gone by
since the day I hitchhiked into the city
and you picked me up

I was probably just a blip on the map
on the side of the road
waiting for something no one could give
when you stopped and said "get in"

Two years later we were living together
in an apartment in Cambridge, Mass.
65 Inman if I remember correctly

We had driven from California
across Canada going nowhere fast
the highway disappearing under
someone else's car

It hurts to laugh or maybe to cry makes more sense
there's a church bell ringing the break of day
you're singing in a chorus in a church on 5th Avenue
we're in New York now, 216 E. 10th,
between 2nd & 1st Avenues, it's 1973
I'm teaching at the other church on the corner where
I once got married, you're studying voice
at the Manhattan School of Music
it's important to get it right for once,
this is not the way things happen

You don't meet someone at random
on the side of the road and live together,

or maybe you do

It's a story we can tell our children
if nothing else
how you picked me up hitchhiking
on the way to San Francisco
and then a few hours later
picked me up again
heading back over the mountain
to Stinson Beach
where both of us lived

Our children shake their heads in disbelief
they can't imagine hitchhiking anywhere
how can you trust the person who picks you up?
but they acknowledge the coincidence
of picking up the same person twice
in the same day
and how maybe that was an omen
we should see one another again
as we did a few days later
at your house up the hill
from the ocean
in Stinson Beach
and then spending the night together
more than once and then moving in together
in the small apartment where I lived
in the house with Greg and Evann Irons
they lived downstairs
and the Veitches lived down the street
la Calle de Ribera
a few steps from the ocean
and Greg died didn't you know he was hit by a bus

in Bangkok
forgive me if I get it wrong

You can tell the story
how (after we broke up) you ran into the street
in New York City
and asked the first person you saw if he wanted
to eat dinner, you had made a big dinner
but the dinner guest never showed up
and you wanted someone anyone to share the food

And this person on the street was on his way to my class
at the church, my poetry class
but he went with you instead,
he took you up on your offer
to have dinner in our old apartment,
and you ended up getting married
and having three kids

It's possible all you have to do
is say hello to someone
and your life will change
in ways you can't imagine

I was just a person living alone
feeling as estranged from myself
as I'd ever been
when you stopped your car
on the side of the road
and I got in

And being with you
being together
made me whole for awhile
it changed everything in the big
scheme of things
the invisible wave
that washes over our heads
and sends us reeling
onto the sand
two citizens of the planet
sharing a match in the dark

We went to the opera together
and I stood in the back
the only ticket available
I went to the church on 5th Avenue
and listened to you sing
and knelt in the pew

Things might have been different if
but I can't finish that sentence
there's a light at the end of the tunnel
but I can tell this story all the same

You were just a girl then
with a beautiful voice
I loved listening to you practice
your scales in the small apartments
which we shared

DON'T LOSE YOUR NERVE

Don't lose your nerve or bite your nails down to the bone.
Don't be scared if the words sound different the second time
around. Hesiod said *ate* is the result of *hubris* but what about
miasma, no one knows about that. No one knows the name of the
god of famine or pestilence, the goddess who leapt from the sea
like a dolphin. This isn't an apology, just a statement of intent. I
danced with a Mongolian woman in an after hours club in Lhasa
and threw out my back. There's the aftermath of the storm when
the sky suddenly brightens. Take the word "maybe" to infinity,
the sun sinking below the ramparts. She walks through the hall
with a towel over her shoulders. It's odd to be alone in a hotel
room with a stone for a heart. I admired you from a distance
without daring to speak. There are no consultants, no therapists,
no one to ask for advice. I say something out of place, like "the
royal blood of the Tartars flows through my veins," and you don't
even bat an eyelash. Sometimes there are many friends, often there
are none. You take my arm as we walk home through the cold. A
fire rages in a warehouse in Queens, one firefighter dead.

ATTACHMENT, DETACHMENT

Retrace your inhibitions across the surface of the past

"How much did you sell your house for?" "It's none of your business"

The tomb of Ch'ang Shen is located in Hunan Province

A cabin ("That's where I used to live") on the side of a stream

Not everyone can be in two places at one time

He was attracted to her because she resembled someone he used to know

You can't walk around naked in the park at night

You can't go to Central Park late at night and take off your clothes

I was forbidden to cross the street when no one was watching

It was enough to make me want to take out a restraining order (I was still a virgin) and stop—like a cop ordering me to slow down—(I was speeding)

A closed caption report replaces an ad for a homeowner's loan

Don't wait for the mirror to reflect who you are

We remember where we were when the boat disappeared under the waves

I am he who boarded a plane to Athens (1969) and I am he who
    pauses to catch my breath on the landing (1995)

He tried to be affectionate but she pushed him away

"Solicited" is the word I was thinking of—there are no more trees

A bridge passes over water and connects two places

Can't see what's right in front of me without closing my eyes

She was the only non-Jewish girl in the school

Everyone in the school had dark features except for Verne, the
    blonde girl from nowhere

There was a rumor that a Catholic girl had transferred to the
    school

She wore a cross around her neck and sat in a corner during lunch

My sister was forbidden to go out with boys who weren't Jewish

A picture reaches out to reality but no one can find it

I sat opposite the Catholic girl and watched her chew her food

Nothing exists inside the picture except for a tree and a flower

The ball hit a crack in the sidewalk and bounced into the street

The derelict falls asleep under his blankets near the corner

Fast—you must move fast through the lines of the poem—down
the page—until the words fill your mind with color

In some countries, it's forbidden to spit on the sidewalk

The first time I took the subway, no one touched me or asked me
my name

I took off my socks and put them on the radiator to dry

If you don't lower your emission standards, I mean raise them,
we'll shut down your factory

All other lovers fade in comparison

And now my books are cluttered, my words are clogged

We were taking a bath together in someone else's house

You could say that I leaned back against you in the bath and
closed my eyes

"Don't step on the caterpillars," she says, as we walk down the path

The only thing she left behind was a pair of tweezers

I came to you for the sake of appearances with the tree shadows
lengthening and with conviction I say we have a long life up
ahead, and I say (together) this book is like a prism reflecting
the colors of the morning light, and I can say—unemployed,
unemployable—that I'm looking into the sun with eyes wide
open

The person who wrote this book was once my closest friend

It seems possible to close one book and begin another

You found the book you were looking for—now go find the pine tree

It's possible for two people to be submissive at the same time

I'm not going to even get dressed today, so if you want to fool
    around—just say the word

I think I'm just going to read in bed for awhile, and drink some coffee

The voice of the seashell was not the white noise of the air conditioner

The voice of the seashell does not compensate for the cry of the seagull

The voice of the seamstress was lost in the white mist of longing

Hands reach out tight, taut, and we lift our heads, no makeup

We fall asleep to the hum of the air conditioning unit in the nursing
    home complex across the air shaft

The men under the boardwalk were playing our song

My mother warned me not to speak to strangers, but I didn't listen

The stranger offered me a bag of candy and I couldn't say no

I was walking home from school when this stranger jumped out of the
    bushes and offered me a bag of candy, my favorite kind

Nothing she had done before prepared her for this moment

Saying something is a way of exposing myself to someone I don't
know

What's left of daylight lingers over the tops of the branches

Maybe I'm a better person for keeping my mouth shut

It's hard to take sides when everyone's wrong

I hold my head underwater until my skin turns blue

We close the book and throw away the key

A wolf climbed up out of the mineshaft and bit my finger

The weather lady caved in to pressure to remove her dress

My love is tapering off as we talk one kiss a minute

I need a new soap dish, our clothing looks muddy, the colors have
blurred

DIFFERENCE

There's a difference between being with someone and being
alone, but I can't tell you what it is. There are things I do
when I'm alone that I don't do around other people. But
don't ask me what they are. For instance, I might have a bone
to pick with you over something that happened long ago, but
you wouldn't know it by the things I say or do. Or the way
I swivel my hips in time to the music, an old disco record
hidden away in someone's attic. It seems like a short time
has passed since we woke to the sound of garbage trucks in
the street, and yawned, grateful to be alive, but not really. I
can fell this tree with a single blow of my ax, so stand back.
Splinters of wood float down from the sky and alight on your
skin. The roof of my mouth is parched, but we must ration
the water if we expect to get out of here in one piece. There
are still some things I want to do in this life, but don't ask me
what they are. Prague, Berlin, Vilnius, Odessa—some cities
I want to visit. Drive up the coast, Bolinas to Point Reyes.
Walk the Malecón in La Paz, one last time.

ECONOLINE

You can't get any higher than
you've already been
before gravity pulls you back
to earth,
and splits you open.

I'm not the type who lies awake worrying
about nothing. Tell her I was here and that I'll
be back later. Call me when you get home,
why don't you?

Desired effects through forced juxtapositions.
Small talk with strangers. The end of something
that never began. The beginning of something
that always ends the same way.

These are the bones of the fallen angel.
If you ask me what happened I'd say
you were wrong. I could say
"this has gone on too long"
and mean almost anything.

The last time I saw her was
in that little restaurant in Brooklyn where they
sell muffins and soup. The one where I fell on my face
and sprained my wrist. A hidden camera caught it
all for posterity.

I paraphrase something someone else
once said. I put it into my own words, so to speak.
Oscillate. Cataclysmic. A scar on the heart.

A woman in a beehive hairdo leans over my desk.
What happens next is not up to you.

A lot depends on the place where you were born.
What your parents did, what they encouraged
you to do. Someone called and said that
his neighbor was harboring fugitives.
"Don't tell them I told you,"
he said, and hung up.

Belief in a weight-loss program
is half the battle. Like when you get
down on your knees and pray for rain.
The train was derailed and the detainees
filled the station. Is it possible to defecate
in the corner of a cage?

I can feel the chill of desire in my wings.
A woman folds her laundry, *gripping*
the clothespin between her teeth. We'll know
each other better after we've lived together
a few days.

Some people dye their hair purple or let it grow
down to their waists. No clothing is appropriate,
I mean not to wear anything makes more sense.

You arrive at your own conclusion
without obfuscation or lies. The exit sign
blinking above the door to the bar
is different from the light in the window
at the end of the street.

I put my hand on your face in the darkness,
but it wasn't you. This is the cabin on the side
of the mountain where we spent the night.
I'm sorry it ever happened.
It never did.

Here's the fence where the strikebreakers
were trapped in 1949. Here's the courtroom
where the union leaders were convicted
of arson.

There are no homilies more brilliant than
eternal perdition. A dog might speak
in a human voice. Someone on the street
is waving a white flag. I'm driving through
the fog: visibility two feet.

ONE FOOT OUT THE DOOR

Maybe life can be defined by the things
you didn't do. The days of amnesty, a pin-up
on the door of the locker, the combination
safe and all the pleasure that comes from
staying indoors when the sun is shining.

"At its apex," you might say, describing nothing.
For once in your life you're at a loss for
words. There's a new library, named after yours
truly, at the dark end of the street. Located between
the dump and the cemetery, just so you know.

SIXTY-FOUR (PLEASURES)

"Will you still need me?"
    —The Beatles

A secret cigarette between classes on a balcony,
Sex in the morning, floating on my back
In the ocean at Maui followed by a mai tai
On the beach, thinking itself a kind of pleasure
That resembles floating, or being drunk (bartender,

Can you bring me another?), another sunset
And the pleasure of waking with the birds
Singing at the window, the pleasure of poetry
Mixed with pain which seems to grow stronger
As time passes

Like giving birth to something that never existed,
Listening to music with my eyes closed
As I drift into a moment of time—
A long train ride along The Hudson
And night coming on.

UP CLOSE AND PERSONAL

The Last Chance Bar is never not open. Don't come down
hard on me if you can't get in, and don't spill your drink on
the rug. You were caught in the crosshairs, but it's never too
late to escape. Yesterday's police blotter didn't mention your
name. You were born in the shape of a bird or a flower. You
write your name in the frost on the glass. There's no time to
waste, one person's desire feeds on another. People in prison
have a long time to ponder their mistakes. But aren't they
already locked inside their heads? The movie ended before
we had a chance to sit down. The pension fund is down to
its last dime. Sometimes the intangibles don't show up in
the box score. And maybe you wake up thinking you're not
alone. Maybe you think this is someone else's problem.

DARK STUDY

for Bill Berkson

There's something we don't know about that's happening elsewhere

A photo by Weegee of a corpse on the streets of Paris

An emergency call from the school nurse went unheeded

All my belongings in one suitcase—how can I help you today?

Add -er to an adjective when you're comparing two objects or people

It looks good on the page but when you read it aloud something
goes wrong

Matches used once may be bartered for tallow

We can trade identities for a few hours and you can feel what it's
like to be me

You can take the initiative and lean out the window until your
hair touches the sidewalk or you can build a moat around
yourself and never touch bottom

Maybe abstraction sounds the death knell to the colloquial
stammer, a tightening of the windpipe as the muffler explodes

A boat passing under a bridge or a woman kneeling at the edge of
the shore

The cars passing in the opposite direction dim their lights when
they see me coming

Possibly you can forget about your own needs for the moment

Maybe I have a brain inside my head after all

We go to bed early and wake with the sun

The sun comes through the curtains like the plague, and we open
our eyes

I slammed the door, boarded the subway, and never looked back

I crossed out what you said before you said it, without thinking twice

The cranberry juice left a stain on the sheet

All new arrivals are cautioned to stay indoors after dark

They built the boardwalk so the old people can sit in the sun, but
when the sun goes down everyone and their mother disappears

A minute feels like an hour, a day is longer than a year

You better turn on the defroster if you want to see through the
windshield

The animal fled into the woods on the other side of the road

Patches of ice float down the windshield in slow motion

All the shadings (equanimity, desire, abandonment) that never add up

Half-sentences mixed with half-truths, complacency and error—is
that your real hair?

It doesn't matter where you were born or where you were going

The suspect climbs down the fire escape and disappears through a
	hole in the floor

Someone too drunk to remember stumbles by under your window

It was before the days of radio and everyone played their own music

Some poets went to brothels, caught diseases, eventually died

Step back from the path and look at yourself, feigning innocence

Turn your back on the javelin while it's still in the air

If I had a hammer it would work both ways, from the center to the
	interior, and out into the open

"But there are no more jobs in the city—we must return home to
	the countryside"

It's her word against mine (if only the trees could speak)

We walk through a cemetery and read the names on the stones

A horse is like a large dog, but with different habits

Memory lingers on, but the distinguishing marks are a blur

The party isn't even half-over and already numerous guests have
	passed out on the living room rug

What you wanted was right in front of your eyes, but you didn't
see it

It's hard to know what you want when something's being given to
you

You can see your whole life pass in front of you in a few minutes

The milkman comes to the door in a horror movie from the 1950s
but no one's home

We park the car at the end of the cul-de-sac and listen to the
birds in the top branches, while the songs on the radio curdle
around us in the stillness

They came to my door with a warrant, but they didn't find anything

They looked under the bed but all they found were a few ghosts

There are tears running down the face of the statue

Rain falls on our eyelids, but we don't wake up

It's a long pilgrimage into the bowels of the earth until you hit
rock bottom

It was like a miracle to see the statue of the Virgin Mary shedding
tears

You never know who you might meet when you walk down the
street

Pride is the same as desire, on a different planet

I'd like to write an epiphany to the saints, but who are they?

Midge, Molly, Maggie, Mickey and Marge

POEM

Things turn old quickly in this life if you're not
careful. A few days ago I burned the back of my
hand on the stove and now the skin is peeling
off. Happily there's another layer of skin beneath
the layer that was burned, otherwise what?

An angel flies overhead and descends on my
shoulder and I close my eyes and everything
that ever happened to me passes through
a filter until there's just a blank page floating
in space. That's what I want. My head, empty

at last, like the end of a ticker tape parade,
layers of confetti covering the street. And now men
with brooms attack the piles of trash left over by
the people who came to the parade. Foreign
dignitaries, the mayor, the police commissioner.

Empty.

ONCE

Once I took mescaline and drove a car down a road in the
country. I got hung up watching the road disappear beneath
the car and didn't notice whether I was in the proper lane.
Happily, I wasn't going far, and I didn't see any other cars
coming from the opposite direction, though perhaps the
drivers were smart enough to stay clear of me, and I just
didn't notice them. It was almost a miracle to arrive where
I was going, stop the car on a dime in someone's driveway,
turn the key in the ignition and get out. There was a musty
sweet odor in the air, a pie cooling on the windowsill, and
the murmur of water in a nearby stream. The frogs were
chirping, the birds were on the wing, a parrot in a cage
was saying "Repeat after me," over and over again, and my
girlfriend was sipping a Dewar's on the rocks at the dining
room table, taking it all in.

NO TRESPASSING

The street goes to sleep early. The store owners close up their shutters before it gets too dark. The streets are deserted after seven in the evening. Most people build gates around their houses. Most people have complicated security arrangements. If an alarm goes off, four or five cops appear within minutes.

The olives on the side of your plate—who will eat them?

Famous last words: "I'll be there in a few minutes." But of course, no one arrives when they say they will. There's always an excuse like "stuck in traffic" or "the alarm didn't go off."

Refer to something outside yourself that never happened.

Is the pressure back on? As far as I know, it was never not off. Stress-related illnesses have doubled in the last few years, not only in this country but everywhere. The stores close down well before midnight. Most people are afraid to go out after dark. There are gates and barbed wire encircling the private houses on the edge of the city. Most people seek out relationships for security reasons, while love gets lost under the dashboard with the cigarette lighter and the parking tickets. You have to pay for a ticket, otherwise they'll suspend your license. And then you'll be nothing but a burden on society, and your friends.

My feet are wet from walking in the rain.

I always read the label on the pill bottle before I take the pill, just to make sure it's the right pill. Sometimes I can't remember if I took the pill five minutes after I did. So young—in the picture he's standing outside the house in the country with a beard and she's pregnant. It's good for the skin, you can roll it on when no one's looking.

We need new frogs to decapitate for our experiment on reflexes.

She came up behind him and said something he didn't want to hear. All the rain can't wash it away, can't wash out the stain. "You say you have some hang-ups and you're going to get help, and I say...." She comes up behind me and whispers something in my ear, something forgettable.

People with masks run towards us between the headlights.

I tried to put the past behind me and then your letter arrived out of the blue. "Acute dysentery" you wrote, and it all came back.

A game of chance on an invisible grid.

Fate asked me what I knew, but I didn't answer. She greeted me as if I were a stranger: I'm sorry, I missed your name. The pine needles are resplendent in their fragile beauty. Everything is up for grabs (except you).

No one will find what's hidden in the closet.

The spaces between my lips and hers. We could kiss for a long time without opening our mouths. We could stand on the steps of her house and grind our lips together endlessly without even touching. Kisses that went on forever, and later, the way one button of her blouse might be opened, and then another. All the blood rushes to the tips of my fingers. The button had to be squeezed through a tiny opening. And then what? Could one simply get to work on the next button? And how many were there anyway?

Rain down on me, through the forest of trees, and melt my feelings.

I was caught in the revolving door again, trying to think about what mattered and what didn't, who I loved and who I still loved but only from a distance. All these thoughts occurred in the split second or two it took me to go around in a half-circle, from the hotel lobby and into the street. It was a street in a medium-sized city where I didn't know anyone and I was there on business. It's possible that you hear what you want to hear and reject the rest, but vigilance, I wrote in my notebook, if anyone cares, is the price of survival. As on a holiday we might eat unleavened bread, we might hide the bread, as my father did, and the person who found it would get a prize.

Our tools are blunt objects, bloodstained and ephemeral.

I was born in Lebanon Hospital in the Bronx, 174th Street and the Grand Concourse. My parents met at a singles resort in the Poconos. Talking, touching, seeing can mean different things to different people. The clouds move across the sky, decorously, as if no one cared.

It's later. The reverse of memory. No platitudes or lies. You want this hole not to exist? Then fill it.

The god of improvement came down from heaven. It's not like he's going around giving people advice for free. You have to go directly to the source if you want his help. You have to make an appointment. At first, no one knew where to find him. There was a rumor that he traveled at night in a horse and buggy. When you expected him to be there he showed up somewhere else. But everyone needs some kind of improvement and the god of improvement has the right answer if you know the right question. Pocahontas stubbed her toe and was rushed to the emergency room but John Smith shot himself in the foot and no one cared. The people of history come out of the woodwork with cameras to take pictures of the people in the present so they can show them off when they return to the land of the dead.

I ride up the coast with the windows open.

It's unbearable to lose face. How can I show myself in public? He entered the classroom and I couldn't keep a straight face. I mean—is this someone's idea of what a teacher really looks like? It looks like when he got up in the morning there was some clothing on the floor and he just picked it up and put it on without thinking. The same clothing he was wearing all week or something. Wrinkles. Obviously this guy needs some help around the house. This is our first lesson in history: the house, and who were the first great lovers? Achilles and Patroclus are high on my list. We think of the first time the lovers met and walked under the trees. And now they don't even sleep in the same bed.

All you have is your own body and the stars to light your way.

It's an even playing field out there, and the god of improvement isn't cheap, but he often says something that changes your life, like when he told me how what I wanted was right in front of my nose and I didn't see it. So I opened my eyes and looked and there it was, just like he told me.

Pull your chair closer to the table so you can eat your food.

There are other gods who try to suck you into their orbit. They hold up signs with your name on it, like limo drivers at an airport. They promise to massage your neck and shoulders—and why stop there?—if only you'll follow them into the forest, down the path to the clearing, all the pine needles and the sunlight through the tops of the trees. Sometimes the "clearing" is just a metaphor for something else, and once you get sucked in it no longer matters. The point is that you're there, and that the gods are standing over you, walking tall, pointing a finger in your direction. All you know is one thing: how to kneel at their feet. And that is all you need to know in this life.

(My grandfather praying in the back of his grocery on the Lower East Side, c.1910.)

It's time to settle into my lawn chair and watch the grass grow, if you know what I mean—a boy on a dance floor steps on the young girl's toes—it's like the trailer for an old movie that won't go away—and now he leads her back to her chair—his hair covers his eyes and he can't see anything—and what could he say if he could and who cares?

You look at my hand as if you were seeing it for the first time.

The talking heads on the radio are speechless for a change. Even the person on the street, when asked, hangs her head in shame. It's not like there's anything to get excited about in the long run, a pair of tweezers on the kitchen table, a few false hopes.

Not to be confused with the other who entered the back way, the one who was here all the time but didn't speak.

It was written in a voice no one could understand. What she said, if it was a she, took my breath away. Felt faint, momentarily, and looked the other way. Then it hit me: I was only half a person and the other half of me was dragging behind. All the flowers growing along the side of the road had withered in the heat and a storm cloud was gathering on the horizon. Someone was stuttering.

THE SURVEY

for Nell Del Giudice

The survey is in, let's add up all the numbers.
Now that we know how everyone feels we can
make a fresh start. Sometimes there's a big contrast
between old and new. You react to something
in the past by going to the opposite extreme. You
make up for your mistakes by going in another
direction. It could be that the new is the same
as the old, but at least for a while it "seems" different.
Soon enough the new becomes the old and the guy
in the outdoor restaurant under the palm trees
with his back to the ocean is singing a song by the
Eagles, while the waitress brings us a plate of
mahi mahi and some girls in hula skirts begin dancing
on a stage and someone throws a tomahawk into
the side of my head which is why I look strange,
talk strange, and am having what's known in some
circles as a bad hair day, but which for me is just
business as usual.

I WROTE THE BOOK

I wrote the book and now it's gone.
It was not as if I was saying goodbye to a person.
It was just words, after all, on a piece of paper,
bound together with other words.
The fact that I wrote them didn't matter any more
since the "I" in question was a different person
than the person I am now. Hard to believe,
isn't it, that not long ago we were hitching a ride
outside Indianapolis in the rain. But that's
what happens when you're lost in the fog of time,
and the geese are heading south in warm weather.

WRITTEN IN STONE

It's important to have an opinion about something before it
gets too late and the world—your immediate surroundings—
blows up in your face. But if you move too far from the
point of origin there's always a chance you'll get lost. And
then you'll need to ask someone directions: which way is up,
and can I buy my ticket on the train? The conductor comes
around and collects everyone's money. There's the chance
that if you fall asleep someone will rifle through your suitcase
and take all your prescription medication and some of your
underwear and socks. An extra pair of socks comes in handy
on winter nights. Even a pair of socks with holes in them.
If you don't have any socks, then a pair with holes is better
than nothing. Don't ask me about the underwear. As far as
wearing someone else's underwear, you must proceed at your
own risk. Meanwhile, the dining car is open, and the ice is
melting on the lake. The last time I went ice skating I fell on
my back and hurt my wrist. I wanted to impress someone
with my athletic skills, but I ended up sitting on the sidelines
with my arm in a sling. It's not the worst fate—sitting in the
shadows, like a wallflower, while everyone else is having fun.
Eventually someone will approach you—a total stranger—
and ask you to dance. You can smell the tobacco on his jacket
and a kind of lilac-scented cologne as you bite into the flesh
on the side of his neck. Soon the dance will be over and
he'll offer to make you a cup of hot chocolate, or something.
There's always a "something" that follows small talk, or a
dance, and at this point you must show your true colors. You
can hold him at arm's length or push him into the line of
traffic, a homicide made to look like an accident.

MANY TIMES OVER

I fill a bucket with cold water and splash it on her face

They left the getaway car under the bridge, but two days later he
was back in the slammer

The tip of the Matterhorn appears out of nowhere

This is the place where I draw a line in the steamy night

This is the steamy part, where everyone embraces someone they
don't know

I swam across the Bosphorus, but no one noticed

Get down on your knees and pull out the weeds

Perhaps you can set things right with a musical interlude, a prelude
by Bach or a symphony by Mahler

The ice cubes scatter around her as she falls to the floor

This office is closed until further notice

There's a first time for everything I want to discover it for myself

The truth comes in increments belly up on the surface

Soon everyone will start singing, a chorus of wood nymphs,
beneath the tympani and strings, taking us to a place where no
one recognizes us for the things we do, our complacencies, our
delusions, the rings of Saturn under a full moon

It's possible you won't even recognize her when you see her in the
   flesh

Her body fell out of the sky and landed in my arms

A game of spin-the-bottle—count me in for the next round

You can find someone else to do your dirty work

The naked ballerina had her hand on the pulse of the century

Better vacate the premises if you know what's good for you

It goes on like this even when no one's looking

You don't know me but I'm right downstairs and I wonder if you
   have a minute

The windmill disappears through the rear-view mirror

The harbor of memory is filled with displeasure

We have to pay a toll before we go in

An alarm goes off in your head and you snap to attention, like a
   private in the army who was reported missing

You roll down your window and hand over your license

It was necessary to take the animal to the pet hospital for a shot

Add up what you don't know and see where it gets you

A movie played backwards, *The Manchurian Candidate* or *High Noon*

It was dark when the deer crossed the road in the fog

A question mark is appropriate at the end of a sentence

The sign says DETOUR, we have to turn at the next light

There's a troll beneath the bridge who kidnapped your sister

Come in out of the cold, you said, and I did

Financial services and health care (soaps, body oils, bath salts, creams), not dishonest but stupid (broad chest, prominent nose) as if anyone cared

An inch of sunlight passses through the tops of the trees

A two day leave of absence is more than anyone needs

The water is flowing under the bridge, literally speaking

The drifter's laughter melts into the dark

You say you live here but no one's home

The blades of the kitchen knives are shiny in the sunlight

I sip some cider and listen to the birds

If someone wants to find me all they have to do is call me up

Order me a Glenlivet on the rocks if you will

"In the long scheme of things"—but I hate that phrase

I was thinking about someone else for a second and closed my eyes

I live in the Royal Roost with my rabbit named Clementine

We seem to have fun spilling holy water into the latrine

Blame can be passed from one person to the next

I should have been smart enough to know what was up, but I wasn't

Maybe you're more like me than you think

You can pass out in the backseat of the car in the rain

The bullet enters someone else's body by mistake

If you get seasick, I have some medicine in my cabin

Here we are in Chicago, of all places, the back room at Danny's

If someone asks you what happened tell them you don't have a clue

A street musician in the subway was playing our song

You can see your face reflected against the backdrop of earth and sky

You can say that you hold up the sky with both hands

Now I can be happy, or something—it doesn't matter

The people on the street glide by in slow motion

When I think about the past I get hungry all the time

The voices in my head are calling your name

Everyone applauds as we cross the finish line

Two feet on the running board, a blaze of light over the bay

THE NEW TESTAMENT

Sometimes only a loincloth
covers the lower part
of his body but no one is
telling him that nakedness
is a sin, or a lie, no one is lying
to him, or lying beside him
in the dark, removing the loin-
cloth or fig leaf from the lower
half. There are dogs
barking outside the sandwich
bar, and a parrot is on display in
the lobby of the Marriott, locked
in a cage for everyone to see.
If I could see in the dark
I would tell you the difference
between the animal and the vegetable,
the nameless and the virginal, those
who rove the streets and estuaries,
their limbs exposed to the elements,
and those who stay at home behind
gated windows and tinted glass.

GHOST RIDERS IN THE SKY

It was like a scene from a movie
starring Fred MacMurray and Vincent Price:
"But I bought you everything you own,"
the character in the movie says, stumbling
out the back door. Some people say
that "the path to satisfaction may lead
almost anywhere," but when the boat
stops in the harbor you better get off.
My consultation fee is $5 an hour, on a
sliding scale, but if you pay for it out of pocket
it's twice as much. More people claim
they act without thinking and pay the price.
If all the motels are full we can always sleep
inside the car. It's preferable to sleeping
on the beach or in the subway. Sleeping on
a subway platform is not my idea of a good
time.

It's always summer where you are and a man
is singing a song about Margaritaville against
a backdrop of ocean and sky. "Some people
say," the singer tells us, "there's a woman
to blame," and then he pauses, "but no," another
pause, "it's my own damn fault." A new
beginning is not a bad idea. It's no one's
fault if you can't see the sky through the tops
of the trees. Once I sat in a room and pretended
to be invisible. "Pass the tabasco sauce,"
I said, but you didn't hear.

This music is my subterfuge, I can turn
it down if you like. It's possible to confuse
two people in your head at the same
time. It's also possible to drink a whole
bottle of wine in one sitting (you leave the
party and pass out at the foot of the stairs).
The party goes on without you but it's not
like you're missing out on anything by not
being there. Let your mind go blank
for a moment and her face appears. A chance
meeting on Elm Street between the Quick
and the Dead.

EVERY PASSING STRANGER

Sometimes you have to twist someone's
arm to get them to do your bidding. Even
basic understanding of a situation depends
on brute force. Pay attention to the details:
"She sipped her tea like a pigeon," and so
forth. The aim is to blame others for everything
that went wrong. Wait till your subscription
runs out and see what you missed. Things
got interesting as soon as you left the room.
Aviator glasses. Dead flowers in a carafe.
Perhaps she was playing at being in love.
All my cards are/were on the table. No point
in pushing the panic button before time runs out.
No reason to pull the plug or hedge your bets.
The Homecoming Queen is taking a breather
on the verandah. There's a jack in the trunk
if you get a flat. You can always show up
at the last minute like the flim-flam man
and make your excuses. It's time to remove
your crinoline, shake off the cobwebs, and bask
in the sun. The radar gun is on the blink: how fast
were you going? It's important to step on
the gas when you pass through the intersection.
The demons retreat into their hovels,
shouting bloody murder, and life dwindles
down to a few precious minutes, enough
time for a double espresso at the No-Name
Bar, if that's your want.

DONATELLO

1

You can preserve your modesty by keeping your
clothing on when you take a bath, even though the
doors are locked and no one's watching. It's another
thing to go swimming in the nude in broad daylight.
Everyone does it. Only you, locked in your room, making
mental notes about the dust in the air, are denying
yourself the pleasure of feeling the ocean on your
skin. It's important to drink the water itself, or so they
say, the water in which you are immersed. It's important
to stay under as long as possible.

2

A notice from the post office arrived when you were
sleeping. You can press a button and erase everything,
all the days of your life. There was an antimacassar
on the arm of the sofa, but I erased that also. There was
an out of order sign on the door of the restroom
written in invisible ink.

Objects might be arranged like facts on a silver platter.
Any combination of objects and facts adds up to something
different. I took off my clothes in the cold on the side
of the road. If my parents never met I'd never be born.
Or something. Someone would be born in my place.

3

Once I took a train from Paris to Barcelona. I left Paris
on August 1, the time that all Parisians leave for holiday
in the south. As a result, I had to stand the whole way.
When I reached Barcelona I went to a bar and ordered
a bottle of milk. I stood at the counter and drank one
bottle of milk after another. Then I went to a hotel and
slept for 24 hours. Why am I telling you this? Please
nod your head if you're not interested or don't want to
listen. I can always replay the scene in my mind
for my own pleasure. That's what I do.

4

Back to the cabin
I don't want to go back

that's what it was
indented   being alone

Never to wake up in the same
way, not us

The other half of pleasure
is never going back

disorder of surface, counter, glass
half of the battle is never leaving

Craving for what lightness
the shadow forsakes

I went back, going back
no one's home, no one can

5

For a dollar and change
you may steal a kiss. We
stand on the periphery
until it's time to leave.
Then we kiss—it's like
having sex with your boots
on, or in a dream—the
train departs and you're
not on it. Alone, in the station,
now that the train has gone—
I'll kiss the first person
I see on the back of the
neck, in a car. Shall we
share a taxi? Sometimes
it's better to kiss and tell,
with eyes wide open—but
please don't bite. The
last time we kissed you
left bite marks on my neck.

6

Tested positive for steroids and won the race.
Or dreamed I was the big winner and sprinted across
the goal. Or thought, as I touched bottom, that
I was weighed down by false promises,
wrapped in a cement kimono,
no context—no contest.

She registered in the hotel under an assumed name
and turned on the bath. He rests his head in his hands,
lost in thought. They propped a ladder
against the wall of the burning tenement,
but no one was home. I tell my children
the story of the shoemaker and his wife.
The shoemaker was happy when the elves
brought him leather.

7

My brethren
have removed their
boots to the corner store

not out of politeness
but for the intrigue
of barter

The touring ice-skating
champion of the world
listens to Nirvana
in her locker

I was born in the middle
of a war but my father
stayed home

8

We were walking down a blind alley
that was someone else's history. There's
the synagogue where I was bar mitzvahed,
covered with graffiti. The streetlights
come on in the evening as the sun goes
down over the tops of the trees. He wanted
to say "like broken arrows" but I stopped
him in his tracks.

The suspect sat in the police station
with his hands in his lap. We lived out our lives
in a subdivision on the road to the airport.
It was you all the time, but no one knew it,
the shadow your body makes on the sides
of buildings and the tops of cars. It was
your shadow intertwined with another
on the shade.

The words turn their backs on you when
no one's looking, but all you can do is close
the door and throw away the key. All you
can do is slam the door in my face!

9

A veldt of stars on black velvet, my wildest dreams.
Our attitude was changing but our debt to the
past continued, following the ripples until they
disappeared beneath the surface. A groundswell
of misinformation, two people kissing on the
beach. It's better to be excluded ("is this seat
taken?") than sit in silence waiting for someone
to come. Some nights I can hear the footsteps of
the people in the apartment upstairs. Music—a party—
the bossa nova—do you want to dance?

10

Let me interrupt my thoughts
to bring you a special
news bulletin. I stubbed my toe

on a rock, but no one's going to cut it off.
A blanket of white snow, a pedestrian
crosswalk, the drawbridge over the Volga.
What happens next is not up to you.

"Come as you are" they said, but who would dare?
Just step off the curb with your eyes shut
and see what happens. The gold rush ended years ago
and a lot of people I know lost their pants.

It's mysterious how you might spend your day
accomplishing more than you have the right to do
without ever breaking a sweat.

You fall asleep with the light on like you did
when you were a kid. I stayed up late reading
when I should have been sleeping. Horse bolts out
of gate and passes the rail in a blur. There was
no time to spare so I split without paying
the bill.

Lock the door behind you when you go
out if you don't mind. The alcohol content
of his blood was over the limit. He wrapped
his car around a tree and hurt his knee. Your
presence is eagerly awaited, nowhere
and everywhere.

11

I step back from the edge with the wind
in my face. A kind of vertigo sets in, alone in bed,
ocean at window, seagulls on the roof.
You can lean your elbows on the tablecloth
for all I care. Footprints of cat in snow.
Tide coming in.

I saw two people naked in a car. A dropping-
off point where the water doesn't move
between your knees. I remember each lie
as if it were yesterday. The bells of St. Mary,
bright and airy.

The house is hidden in the folds of the trees.
I wouldn't say it if it wasn't true. You might
as well discard your baggage before you cross the

border. There's no telling what you're going to find
on the other side.

As a kid I read "The Pit & The Pendulum" by Poe.
In my spare time, I played with a neighbor's dog.
Slept on an air mattress and listened to the chains
on the cars in the snow. A woman with cracked
fingernails comes to my rescue, but there's
nowhere to go.

12

I can hear the rumble of trucks taking migrant
workers to the abandoned orchard on the edge of
town. It's there that the movie ends, and no one gets
punished for the crimes they didn't commit. But
maybe being on probation isn't the worst case scenario
we were hedging our bets would happen given
the circumstances and the circumstantial evidence
didn't exactly help our cause either. I'm skirting
the issue again. Last night's coffee grounds, a purple
flame. We could sleep the lie of forgetfulness
and never wake up. There's the key to the future
we know nothing about. Names of cities, the fork
in the road, human voices, original sin.

13

A person might be incarcerated for parking
his or her car at a broken meter. It was right
in front of your nose but you didn't see it.
The water is up to your shoulders, but you
keep on sinking. *The seams in their pockets,*
the hems of their trousers.

The person I was kissing was reported missing.
The kiss might last a lifetime or end in a minute.
A can of paint thinner was left out in the rain.
The person I was kissing had changed her name.
That was last year, but this is now.

We read about an initiation rite where "the candidate
is subjected to an operation in which his body
is dismembered and his internal organs are removed."
We make lists of astronomers: Newton, Galileo, Kepler.
We say: "In order to protect my mother, I'll kill myself."
We stop for gas at a Texaco station on the road
between Albany and Troy. We go to a doctor who says
"the cough is all in your head." We say, in unison,
that "an island is a body of land surrounded by water."
We cross out what we wrote the night before. We
leave early to avoid the traffic. We fall asleep
in our wet clothing on the side of the road.

14

One might as well pee on the sidewalk
and hope that no one reports you
to the police. Meanwhile, someone complained
about being bitten by red ants.

I'll arrange for you to be transferred
to another department if you like. You're
fired, laid off. I'll call you if I need you.
Why don't you call me? My number's
unlisted.

I think it's time to explore the sewers
of Paris once again. You can get a guided tour
if you arrive before dawn.

When I return from the land of the living dead,
I'll call you up. The last time I saw her
was on the escalator in Bed, Bath & Beyond.
She was going to the basement to buy
some linen, and a few new pillows.

15

Here's a videotape of naked people dancing
around a bonfire. Sometimes it takes years
to find something you've lost. Sometimes you
let something go and you regret it later. It didn't
take long for you to realize that you made
the wrong choice. I lose something briefly
and then I find it again.

A person withdraws into his or her shell.
Rings around Saturn, a cluster of stars.
Joy is not the same as happiness.
Desire: procurement of pleasure, avoidance
of pain. *Travail attrayant*, pleasurable
work. It's not difficult to read another
person's mind. The soundtrack continues,
though the screen goes blank.

You can say something one minute
and deny that you said it, without thinking twice.
The words disappear like smoke into the ether.
We commit the words to memory so we can
repeat them later.

The habits of a lifetime can be changed over night.
You can't say my words were written in stone,
only to be revoked the next day. The epicenter
of the earth consists of a few broken twigs
and branches. According to the weather lady, the
chance of rain is less than zero.

You can take out your anger on someone
you don't know and maybe you'll apologize
afterwards as the train goes around the bend.

"Don't make promises you can't keep,"
was a favorite song. It seems to punctuate
the mood of the day, never the same.

Words overlap like waves, contractions, waves.
We read the words of warning on the label.
We open the can with our teeth when no one's
looking.

Traumatic experiences break through the protective shell.
I'm sorry you had to go out of your way to get here
but now that you're here
why not make yourself at home.

Maybe if you break something
into little pieces you can restore it without trying.
I can see a cloud from the balcony, a dot on the
horizon. I can see you in the distance,
like a tornado, coming my way.

HUNGRY GHOST

A gram of desire for breakfast;
gruel for lunch. Dinner on the town,
some place not too fancy.
Who'd you call cheap?

POEM

You can fire the fusillades
over my head, for all I care. And
cut my body in half on an empty
stage. My name used to be
'Boxcar Bertha' but now I am one
with the scum of the earth.
You can carry me away from
the uprising with my head bloodied,
and my arm in a sling. But
if they ask you, 'they' meaning
the people who report such things
to the denizens of the deep,
say I was smiling through closed eyes,
though I couldn't speak, and
the blood on my cheek was the color
of pomegranate.

READING GU CHENG

Whenever I think of the story of Gu Cheng and how he killed himself and his wife I think of the time I sat on the porch of my apartment in Park Slope with his wife not long before that happened and I think how beautiful she was and if only we could have said more than a few words to one another how lovely that would have been and what an idiot I am for not learning Chinese I had a Chinese girlfriend for seven years and all I knew how to say was hello and thank you and how are you and a few other words. Gu Cheng and I never said anything to one another. He liked to pretend that he didn't know English. He seemed above it all and who was I anyway? Ping made lunch that day and we sat around the table in the living room, and I sat next to his wife to be close to her beauty. But mostly I remember sitting quietly just the two of us on the porch looking out at the garden while everyone else talked inside, maybe Yang Lian was there too. I loved Yang Lian of all the Chinese poets I met when Ping and I were together and I know I'll see him again someday. But it was Xie Ye, the wife of Gu Cheng, who I remember for the half hour we sat on the porch. I had the feeling she wanted not to be in the living room with the other poets and I wanted to keep her company no matter what. I wanted to hold her hand, something, out in the garden. We talked about our children, hers and mine. Then we went inside and had lunch and everyone was talking in Chinese. This is what I think about when I read Gu Cheng's poems.

RITUAL NUDITY

I reconstructed it from memory before
I left for sea. I left for sea and you waved
goodbye from your window. Goodbye to
the light on the linoleum. Goodbye
exit sign. Goodbye footsteps.

Cut into slices. Tottering on heels.
A swarm of analogies (like locusts, like
flies). Parody of copulation, not
your place or "mine." Out of deep need,
the need to talk—make noise, music,
use of different sources (voices),
communication "from my body to other
bodies" no matter who.

Carbon monoxide poisoning "on
the rise" outside Hoboken. The
preposition rests its case. Refer to
footnotes. *Il neige, il pleut.*

THE DESERTED CITY

Here's the door of the church. How much does it cost to
get in? There's the priest at the door with a hat in his hand.
Here's the doctor with a clipboard, listening to your dreams.
Yes, you can pay on a sliding scale, and no, you can't kiss me
on the lips when you say goodbye. You can't even kiss me on
the cheeks like they do in Paris. Strangers, fucking strangers,
they kiss everybody on the street. Sex between doctors and
patients is forbidden, or so they think. There's a toll if you
want to get in, just put your money in the slot. The correct
change, please, there's no money back guarantee. Follow the
directions on the side of the package and you can't go wrong.
They give you the wrong number when no one's listening.
It's not enough money to take anyone to court. Call my bluff
if you don't believe me.

We've been in the deserted city too long.
I dipped my cup in a watering hole and fell on my face.
He was frightened of seeing the elephant's penis.
Place an order at the counter and hope for the best.

PROMISE

I was holding back something I wanted to say.

It seemed like if I said it I might hurt someone's
feelings.

I'm not saying you shouldn't say something
for the fear it might cause someone pain.

Maybe I'm saying that you shouldn't say something
without taking the feelings of the person into account.

There's no point in saying something about someone
for the sake of saying it.

You say something to somebody and that person
tells someone what you said.

You tell someone not to tell anyone what you're
telling them but they break the promise and tell everyone.

You can't assume that anyone, even your closest
friend, can keep a secret.

It was hard to tell anyone what you were feeling
if you thought they would tell what you said to someone
else.

"I promise I won't tell anyone," she said, but it was
just a lie.

You can whisper something in someone's ear and they might repeat it to someone else.

It's not a secret if you tell someone so maybe it's best not to say anything.

Best to keep everything locked inside, until it kills you.

VODKA

The spirit just floated out of the top of my skull like a puff
of smoke and evaporated in mid-air. All the good
feelings.

You can apply the chokehold to someone you don't
like and suffer the consequences. Clogged
roads filled with people running from something they
can't see.

That's where St Vincent's Hospital used
to be. I went there one night when I had a
pain in my chest. And there's the old DVD store,
on Greenwich Avenue, now a hardware store.

(My voice trails off.)

The clothing store on 7th Avenue you
liked, The Colony, now a real estate
office. I used to buy you gift certificates there
for your birthday.

Who you kidding? Mind your manners.
Fork on left, knife on right. That can't be right.

Intelligent people sit in the caboose, but the
daredevils go up front. They want to look out
the window and see what's coming.

Describe the hotel room in perfect detail.

Eclipse the taste of defeat from the night before.

A negation placed before a verb.
Or after.

SITUATION WANTED

Just call me Big Lew, you know where to find me,
down at the corner sucking a smoothie through
a straw.

Now you can smile like any goody two-shoes.
Who knows where he's going
when he leaves the room.

Bend down to tie shoelaces on crowded boulevard.

The tinctures of memory begin to fade
like an old wound.

Nothing but liquids can pass into the stomach.
Think about unity, a thankless task. I stammer
in my excitement. You set the alarm
for three a.m.

Each word sounds different
tongue, mouth, lips. The shape
of the letters, a teabag in hot water.

The old, the young, the miserly.
All of you can get off at the next stop.

I'll take a lie detector test if it makes you happy.
To tell you the truth, I don't have a clue.

My gaze is unblinking, as if there's no tomorrow.

My lips are moist, as if tomorrow
never came.

We live in dream time: expand, contract.

Backseat referendum. Sustenance guaranteed.

ALL SOUL'S DAY

A kiss on the cheek is all you're going to get.
Regressive behavior isn't rewarded much
in these parts. For all I know, the world is flat
like a stale pancake and when you reach
the side of the plate you fall over the edge.
For all I know, there's a snake pit on the other
side of the sky. Something to think about
when you lose your way in the middle of night.

"Elsewhere" isn't a place you can go to
in your dreams. The train jolts to a stop
outside Eureka and everyone gets off. Yesterday
I caused a commotion by airing my dirty laundry
on the banks of the river. It wasn't as if
I said something that would make
a difference, on the contrary
it would be my greatest hope if indifference
set in, like a head cold that won't go away
even when you're alone and the windows
are shut tight, and the person at the other end
of the line is talking to you from twenty years ago,
saying things that were better left unsaid,
even then.

There's no way you can see beneath the skin
unless you cut into it (and then stitch it up).
Even so, an exposed nerve is sensitive
to extreme cold. It was said that, describing
her emotions, she went from hot to cold
at a moment's notice. It was said
that the roof of the house blew off in the storm

when everyone was asleep
and that the bodies were still asleep
(as if they were dead)
when the storm blew over.

Human voices speculate on the market
value of objects no one wants. Commodities,
oddities, luddites, an invitation to the
senior prom, food stamps, martyrdom,
the barn and the silo and the general store which
burned down last year. I remember
seeing the proprietor of the store with flames
shooting out of his head. An ambulance
pulled up and took him to the emergency
room, but the fire raged on.

THE ARTIFACT OF LINOLEUM

Two subway tokens, and
a front row ticket to *Aida* at the Met,

won't get you to first base
with a mongoose named Froggy.

The author of "The Little House
on the Prairie" was on the take,

along with Wonder Woman (the rerun).

A gang of men with no chins
attacked the Swami outside his
home. It had to do (someone said)
with the brie.

Pre-DNA, all you knew were
the symptoms.

A leak from the upstairs toilet.

A little headroom, where before
there was none.

WHEN YOU WORE A TULIP

Lazybones perked up at the sight of her
camisole.

Homer & Jethro pushed the panic button
without thinking.

There was a gimmick
about being two different people

attached at the hip

to two other people
who were born
under the wrong sign.

My skinned knee
was bothering me

so I flagged a taxi
and went to Florida.

Outside influences. Fin
de siècle *sturm und drang.*

I have an ace up my sleeve for when
the bottom drops out. Gas
prices skyrocketing from Carbondale

to Podunk. A soothsayer in your
backyard? Call the body shop

and ask for Fred.

STIGMATA

The man downstairs warns us about the bedbugs in his apartment
and the next day I have big bumps on my arms

There are bugs in the soup among other places

It's no coincidence that Gregor Samsa turned into a bug

Joy and sadness are like sweet and bitter food

The places you visited don't exist when you're not there

The world is a forest filled with wild beasts and poisonous insects

The anesthesia is just wearing off and a nurse is sitting at my
bedside

Maybe when I'm old and blind you can read to me before I fall
asleep

You were sleeping here a moment ago and now you're gone

This is what used to be known as the meatpacking district

It's not a problem (for me) if you want to burn everything you've
written

I put some cortisone on my bites to relieve the itching

The hair stylist on the ground floor claims that the birds on the
windowsill attract rats

I had the sense that someone was following me so I turned the
corner

There's a theory that only the beginning and the end are important

I skipped a few pages to find out what happens at the end

You may read a short summary of the book before you begin

I tried to throw the ball through the hoop, but it went astray

"The self-acknowledged suffering of the disintoxicated is the
subject of this book"

Every word is a verb: to do, to be, to seem

The words are in italics because I'm saying them

My so-called doppelgänger is not my friend

It's a long way down from the roof to the street

Waiting on line at the bank we are simply nobodies

I run out into the snow / but there's nowhere to go

My head is no longer part of my body

When I first started wearing glasses, people called me "Owl"

When I walked down the street people shouted "Hoot! Hoot!"

One word from you and my thoughts begin spiraling

It's hard to know what to do next until you're doing it

My private parts are glowing in the dark

There was a buzz in the audience at the sound of her name, but
   after her performance people looked downcast and filled with
   despair, as if the propensity to feel anything had vanished
   forever in her presence

It feels like there's a nail sticking into the bottom of my foot

Darkness commensurate with discomfort—this style of writing

Self-discipline is necessary if you want to forget something

There's a struggle, never ending, between clinging to something
   and letting go

A stream of water flowed out of my head

You can walk down Gun Hill Road in the Bronx and be
   anywhere

You can stand at the intersection of Gun Hill Road and
   Eastchester Road and remember the past

I can see the light of a taxi in the distance, coming through the
   snow to take me home

You can walk down Lydig Avenue in the Bronx and remember
   your childhood

I cursed at the doctor who wanted to give me a shot

In those days, when you were sick, the doctor visited you in your
    apartment

There's the intersection where I waited for a bus—it's after midnight

Once I took speech lessons to correct my lisp

It's time to leave the party but I can't find my coat

I omitted the sentence you asked me to erase without fear of rain

Long shot of an empty downtown street—coffin-like, unreadable

"We're walking on sunshine—ooh, ooh"

Side effects might include drowsiness or diarrhea

It's important to clean the sink before going to sleep

Sometimes the bugs come out when you're sleeping

The sky is overwhelming but so is the vastness of the sea

We buy a magnifying glass so we can identify the bodies of the
    dead bugs

The dead bugs leave a trail of blood along the sheets

It's hard to touch someone who isn't here

Your call will be answered in the order in which it was received

The dermatologist touches the welts on my skin

The ferry is late and we won't be home

HELLO STRANGER

It's a good time of year to get out
of the city. The canals are open and
traveling is cheap. You can see the stars
behind the tops of the trees. The dance
of blue veils like ripples in a mirror.
The handmade vests of the clouds
embroidered with tiny beads.

Time is up. If you haven't figured out
the answer by now you never will.
(They arrested him in the middle of
the night for stealing a chicken.)
Put on your clothes, they
said, and come downtown.

★

"Memories are Made of This"
was a hit by Dean Martin. The chorus
in the background sang "Sweet
sweet, memories are made of this,"
until finally he woke up and asked
whether he was dreaming.
His penis, we both noticed, wobbled
as he spoke. When the dust
cleared, we could see him
tottering on the edge of the
curb, waving his arms at the
oncoming traffic.

★

"Everything
in the natural
world," he wrote,
"has a counterpart

in the world of the
mind." I open a
notebook
from 1985.

You were lying in
bed on your side with
your back to me
as I walked out
the door.

Etna, Vesuvius,
Zoroaster,
synoptic.

★

My words seem to stand for something else.
In the time it took to speak they had disappeared
from view.

The red coals will protect my spirit from growing
old. If you step on a mine you will explode
like a shooting star.

There's a rumor that nothing can begin

until you arrive. Meanwhile, they serve beverages
and show old movies.

The scene is frozen in
the back of my mind, like
shredded lettuce left out in the cold.

Tell me what the food is like
where you are. Right out of the package
and straight to the heart.

★

Dust on the hem of a petticoat—don't get me started.
Someone you never saw before whispers in your ear.
You better return to the company of the living
before it gets too late. The floor is covered with threads
left over from the people who lived here before.
But the closet is empty, except for a few old socks.

More than I bargained for, someone says.
But compliance with the verb "to remember" throws
us off course. We can't lie down on the shore
and listen to the waves break out of the untrammeled
deep. Even Shelley came up for air, what little good
it did, and went back under.

★

Each generation needs its own music
Each thread needs a hole—but
the button also 'hanging from
a thread'

as it was said—his love
for her lingered long after
she had gone—(he tried to get on
the train
as it was leaving the station)—the music
in my head is in my head. He refused
to express the slightest
regret for his behavior. Each leaf might
be a map of light
in paradise—out the car window
at night. "I'll leave
the light on if you come home late."
Each hand five fingers
waving goodbye at the station—as the train
leaves the station. I'm on the platform
(waving). Each generation needs to say
goodbye to the past.
But the present crumbles in the
hand (like a leaf).

★

It felt like centuries had passed
before we collapsed in each other's
arms. (He tried to be affectionate
but she pushed him away.)

Tell me about the Russian restaurant
on the boardwalk at Brighton Beach.
A child jumped off a rock and disappeared
beneath the waves. She was memorizing
her lines so she could take your place
at a moment's notice. She was waiting in

the wings to make her appearance
on an empty stage.

★

Memories are just accumulations of things
that have acquired meaning over
the passage of time, but the things
that you've forgotten still carry their weight
without weighing you down the way
the things you remember tend to do,
though the opposite might also be true,
and another gin and tonic, no ice, won't
get you through the day,
even if you look in the mirror
and see who's missing, for instance, yourself.

Sorry for staying so close to the perimeter.
It's more fun out in the open, don't you think?
Tomorrow we'll eat yogurt soup and baklava
on the road to heaven.

When someone asks me to make a choice,
I usually say "I'll sleep on it." And I do. I sleep eight
big hours in my king-size bed. It's so big
I can roll over and not touch any of the people
I'm sleeping with. They don't even know I'm there,
if you want the truth.

DURANGO

Cold silent wind on a quiet
evening. Soda crystals,
boiling water. Let's make a fresh
start.

All the dead weight, all the
riffraff, the night
Pecos Pete came to town

in a rickshaw and a volley
of hail the size of tennis balls
fell from the sky. You could

buy some pills from the guy
on the bench in the park.
A nose on his face, unlike mine.
Gin and fizz.

It seems like you can be two people
at the same time, or more. The bowels
of the earth are empty and the
movie theater is closed. What have

we here? A story by Poe.
A shark out of water. The first
microwave. Perpetual dawn.

WATCH ON THE RIND

You fall asleep with eyes wide open. You
learn how to be present when you're not
even there. Miles away, thinking about
something else, but acting like you have
both feet planted on the ground.

Sometimes you have to test the waters
before you go in. That means nothing. You
can float back to earth or step off the carousel
when it's spinning. Either way, you
luck out, and walk away, as if nothing

happened. There's a three month
guarantee for parts before breakfast
but by noon the story changes
and you have to get on your knees
if you want anything. Just sign on the
dotted line until Xmas.

A lopsided score gets the attention of the
pundits, all the usual suspects and their families
and friends gather around the barbecue
pit for Sunday brunch. Don't set off
the alarm just because you smell smoke.
It could be anything. Inflammable pajamas.

Anything.

POEM

Excuse me—you say "excuse me"—and then
it's time to go. You say: "I have to leave"—and you
close the door behind you. (You don't have
to say anything—I can tell you want to go.)   No
one notices that you're gone until it's too late
to do anything. Once you were sleeping in this bed
and now you're not. (The woman turns to the place
where the man was sleeping.) There are too many
moments in the day—"Is this seat taken?" We
make our excuses and leave the way we came.

There was a movie about the executive and the
secretary, they're working late. You can spell
out the obvious, it's all happening behind closed
doors. The office building has been demolished,
I have it on tape. The building was detonated,
we can all go home.

Analyze resistances, say the opposite of what
you mean. The last thing you'll ever do is admit
that you were wrong. It's too risky to say
what you mean, so you say the opposite, you
don't say anything. I read three books at the same
time with two eyes. I stare at a photograph
of Georgia O'Keeffe in the nude.

I came up for the weekend and stayed forever.
It's a buyer's market, meaning it's a bad time
to sell. But I've never owned anything,
nor wanted to. My needs are modest,
by most standards, as far as I can see.

A screened porch where you can read late at night.
A barn with some chickens, maybe.
A couple of sheep.

WHAT IT MUST FEEL LIKE

What it must feel like on the bottom of
the ocean. A harpoon buried in the mud.
Pirate Jenny on the tube.

Sometimes you come up for air
when no one's looking and look around.
Absorb the future before it absorbs you.

Stillness of sonar from nearby sub
showing *Hunt for Red October*
spin-offs

snatches you out of the gloom state
you've been in since she left,
but that was so long ago

it's hard to remember the waves that
came over your head like a bad moon
rising above the deserted downtown

streets, I mean Wall Street where the fat
cats live out their fantasies and the
escorts pile into the backseat.

Smelling salts are useful. Now my head
is clear and resting on the soft pillow
(your stomach). Ooh, I can hear the antacids

at work, hard hats with shovels
tunneling out like an ocean liner
on the ocean floor. These boots

were meant for walking in the
deep end, where no one goes,
and no one knows your name

or where you were born,
small talk around a water cooler
or conversations at a clambake,

the flora and fauna
with their colorful orifices
and twisted smiles.

SONG OF THE DRIFTER

Some ordinary drifter enters the picture. Some
say he fell for the farmer's daughter and
asked the farmer for her hand in marriage.

But if permission wasn't granted and the farmer
forbid the drifter from marrying his daughter,
no doubt the drifter and the underage daughter

would escape after midnight on the back of a horse.
Of such stories songs are written. The horse has a name,
like King or Fritz. The farmer's daughter wipes

the sweat from the horse's brow. She rests her
head on the drifter's back and whispers into the
horse's ear. The horse runs up one hill

and down another, like a pitcher of water
passing from the lips of the drifter to the lips
of his bride as they ride into the night.

Soon the veil of sleep comes over them,
the drifter, the farmer's daughter,
and the horse.

You can play the song over again, how the
drifter showed up one morning and asked the
farmer's daughter for a glass of water.

Little did the farmer know that the drifter
was falling in love with his daughter.
One night, the drifter and the underage

daughter climbed onto the back of a horse,
and rode off. You can request the singer
to sing it again, one never gets tired

of hearing the same story, how the daughter with
green eyes, and the anonymous drifter who looked
like a fish out of water,

hopped a freight train in the middle
of night and hightailed it across the border,
in search of a new life.

FIVE O'CLOCK SHADOW

There's a private party,
and it's going on right now.
If you haven't been invited
there's still a chance that
the guy at the door might let
you in in exchange for a kiss.
But a peck on the cheek isn't
enough. Not in this climate,
where only the comatose
and the vacuous among us have
their day in the sun. My eyes,
yours, a reflection in still
water, what might have been.
Two grasshoppers copulating
under a rock. One step forward,
one step back. Another chorus
of Satchmo singing "Hello Dolly."
I'm going to call room service.
"Room service? I'd like a bowl of
clam chowder and a plate of mahi-
mahi. Hold the lemon." I walk
through the front door and out
the back without thinking
twice. Not only don't I know
anyone at this party, but it's like
I showed up at the wrong address
in a dress and no one cared.
Maybe I'll get into bed with a
bar of halavah and a box of cotton
swabs and call it a day, even
though it's night and the

shutters are closed, all the
slipshod typists have gone
home and the major arteries
are backed up from Perth
Amboy to Troy, hair flying
over the Dead Sea so many
light years away.

ALIEN ABDUCTION

1

The line of least defense has melted away.
If the reviews are mixed, you can always
take the show on the road. Why don't you
get out of your wet clothing and get into bed?
I slap a pad of butter onto a pancake
(figuratively speaking).

The mystery of love was that it was over
before it began. There was always
the chance it would come back
to haunt us in a different way. An animal
in a carrier left on a subway platform
over night. Large scale fortunes, limited
prosperity, opportunities for failure,
nothing to lose.

2

There's something in the climate that's like an excuse
for staying home. Every day something different gets
lost in the cracks. Listen to the sound of things breaking,
the snap of twigs. A cameo in a movie that never made
it to your local theater. Tire tracks embedded on the surface
of space. Unleavened bread broken into pieces and hidden
away. A party where everyone is required to undress
before midnight. A woman with a single tooth in bed with
two men—all ghosts.

3

Someone is cursing and someone else is babbling
to himself and someone is frightened and stares at
her feet. The older people are falling asleep in their
beach chairs as the sun goes down over the horizon
and I'm drinking a pina colada and my left leg won't
move. The boat is at the dock and people are waving.
The women wearing long dresses with elaborate
hems. Every day three people cross the street. A, B
and R are not their names. The sirens on the rocks
are singing to the men in the boats. Smiling like an idiot
when the lights come on.

4

See her as she wades through the rows of desiccated flowers.
See her on the sidewalk as she bends to tie her shoe.
I can see her in the dark turning the pages of a magazine with
pictures of food: coconuts, mangoes. Now I know what the
phrase "hell iced over" means. The driver refuses to take me to
Brooklyn, and who can blame him.

Brackish water cascades from faucet to
cupped hands and then disappears into
drainage system of old-fashioned tenement
apartment. Don't complain.
You can love someone without lying.
You can love someone with equal
intensity. You can sink into the
sickness of infinitude and never
return.

5

There's never been a vaster
deployment of desire than what
happened to me when was
it 1964

and what did we do but stay up
all night and ride in a Saab at dawn
from East 10th Street to Harlem

through Central Park where in a
5th floor apartment the whole
world happened at once
                            with the kids
in the playground out the back window
at lunch time

and Dionne Warwick was singing
"Anyone Who Had A Heart" and I
thought I should walk up the
hill to my job in the library at Columbia

but instead I called in sick and we
stayed in bed while the baby napped

6

Feelings for another person can be a source
of unhappiness. You can see your whole life pass
in front of you in five minutes. Once I leapt
over a puddle and skinned my knee on the

pavement. The cuffs of my pants were
soaked and my mother scolded me. "Take off
your socks," she said, and I did.

It's good to drink a glass of hot milk when you
can't fall asleep. A saucepan on the stove under
a low flame. She parked the car at the station
and waited for her husband to step off the train,
but he never came, never did, never will.

Is an orange orange? A rose red?
I can wear complimentary colors. I can burn
in the sun. Do you want some lotion?
Sorry, I forgot to bring it. I'm drinking a mai tai
and watching the sun go down over the ocean.
The birds sing at my window. The sky is a blur.

7

It's been a long time since I converted libido into
anxiety. Whenever it happened I'd say to myself: at
least I'm not a machine. A machine might be able
to have sex in every possible circumstance. But for me
signing my name on the dotted line was enough. I
pulled up my pants and went to the window. There
was a Burger & Brew on the corner and a bike messenger
eating takeout. I advised you to get dressed immediately
and never tell anyone what had happened. Years later
I must admit I'm only human after all. It's easy to
highlight the halftones when you try to remember
a dream. I stare down the looks of the men who ogle
you on the street and give them the finger when
they're out of sight.

8

Focus your attention on one other person.
You continue to feel love for someone long
after the person has gone. There was some
satisfaction in thinking about the person
who wasn't there, who had said goodbye,
boarded a plane at LaGuardia, and disappeared.
It wasn't as if you were clinging to a feeling
based on something that had happened
in the past, but had submerged yourself
in the feeling until nothing else mattered.
The present didn't matter, nor the street on which
you lived.

9

Nothing grows to fruition without intention. What
you wanted was right in front of you, but you didn't
see it. A woman reclines on a floral cushion behind
a beaded curtain. The conversation in my head is
always one-sided, me talking to a person who never
talks back. An emergency phone call to the school
nurse went unheeded. I tried to climb a hill in the
middle of the night but the dogs began barking. Let's
say I come to you as an Egyptologist, with no strings
attached, simply to lecture on the Great Pyramids of
Cheops. You can identify the type of bird by the colors
of its feathers. A view of the river and the tugboats
(touching dry land).

NEW YEAR'S EVE

You can make believe you saw the forest
for the trees. It's like a disease.

You can call the head honcho on his private line.

You can strum the frets of your Fender until
they bleed.

You can sacrifice a knight for a queen without
thinking twice.

You can sleep on the job in a tow-away zone.

You can pan for gold until your fingers grow
numb or catch the run-off in a styrofoam
cup.

You can toss the dog a bone in your own sweet time.

You can borrow a song from the Preservation
Hall Band.

You can turn off the pilot and plot
your next dream, pick lice from a child's scalp
and whistle in the dark.

You can buy me a drink, Dewar's with ice, but I can't
pay you back.

You can tie a sailor's knot around the trunk of a tree.

You can adjust your shades to block out the light.

POLAR NIGHT

Maybe if you could see yourself
from a distance
you could see what people see
when they see you close up

they can see the canaries and the penguins
and the darts flying through air,
like missiles above a city
only the trajectory is all wrong.

Only the sonnet is wrong,
and the signature on the dotted line,
a pool of light in the puddle
at the bottom of the well.

Maybe if you abandoned the song
and the tubes of the radio went dead
you would rub the hands of a stranger
in the storm.

You would lie on a mattress
with broken springs and take your
swings with your foot
in a bucket.

If you close your eyes tight you
might recognize me if I touch
your skin. The tattoo of a flower
in the shape of a heart.

NEW TRAVELOGUE

I stumbled out of the bushes
to see a deer drink from a pool.
I climbed into the hills above
Berkeley, one step at a time.
I went to Prince Edward Island
where Anne of Green Gables' face
is on the license plate. A hawk
or a condor flew over our house.

I bought a carton of smokes
at the duty free shop in Anchorage.
Took a seconal in Frankfurt
and woke up in New York.
I bothered my friends with my troubles;
I was never (not) alone. I postponed
pleasure until it was almost gone.

I stared out over the North Sea,
waiting for rain. I wandered
through the red light district in Amsterdam
in the middle of night. I rode on
the back of a motorcycle over a mountain
on Christmas Eve.

I floated on my back in the ocean
at Maui. Stared out the window of
my hotel room over the rooftops of
Florence. Took LSD in Paris and sat
on a bench in the Luxembourg Gardens.
Rented a hotel room in Liverpool
but couldn't sleep.

I missed my flight from Madrid to Lisbon.
Found an apartment on the Panhandle
and drank tea in Golden Gate Park.
I was caught stealing at Safeway—I could never
return. A Chinese acupuncturist came to
my house when I threw out my back

and couldn't move. I woke up in an apartment
on 5th Street and listened to the roosters
crow on someone's roof. I visited her
in her house overlooking the ocean and she
let me in. I put out my hand to touch you,
but the bed was empty.

I wheeled a stroller down an icy New
England street. Waited under a canopy
in the rain, but she never came. I stood
in front of a classroom with paint stains
on my shoes. Called the suicide hotline,
but no one answered.

I dropped everything I was doing
and ran into the street. Drove
a car with faulty transmission until
a fire started under the hood. I ate
Indian food on a balcony in Capetown.
I sang karaoke in a bar in Tibet.

Something I meant to say comes back
to haunt me in my sleep. I turn
the key in the lock and call your
name. Her face appears, out of nowhere,
making a shadow on the page. There's
only one stone and it weighs a ton.

THE CONGA LINE

It would seem that I was holding
your hips from behind and that you were
swaying to the music which was
coming from the other room. The
door to the room was open
but no one was entering or leaving.
It was the type of party where people
drifted in, stayed for a few minutes
or a few hours, and then went home.
I had the feeling that I was already
home and that I was holding onto your hips
from behind as we danced around the
room with our eyes closed, bumping
into the furniture while the music
played on. Then someone caught me
from behind and held onto my hips with
hands that resembled claws. I could
feel his breath on the back of my neck
as we circled around the room. There
was someone in front of you, an old man,
your hands on his hips, and as far as I knew
there was someone in front of him,
a young woman with hair down to her waist,
and that he was holding onto her waist
with his withered hands, and that there
was someone in front of her as the line
of dancers snaked around the room
and onto the balcony where the moon was
shining on the tops of the trees in the garden
and you could hear the sea in the distance,
the foghorns that seemed part of the music,

a new instrument, woodwind or strings,
you could hear the voices of the people
singing in time to the music, as if they
had migrated from another planet
and were trying to get the most out of the
pleasures of the new world
in which they had landed almost
at random out of every possible place
in the universe. It's a pleasure to dance,
as much as it's also a pleasure
to stand on the sidelines
and observe the bodies of the people
on the dance floor without feeling envious
or sad, as if something happened
when you were a child to make
you act the way you are now, so whenever
anyone asks you to dance you shake your head,
pretend you're too drunk or tired,
without ever measuring the potential pleasure
of putting your arms around a stranger and leading
him or her across a dance floor, or in the case
of the conga line actually pressing your whole
body into the back of another person,
as if you were fucking that person from behind,
for instance, as some people like to pretend
they're doing while they dance,
as if the idea of dancing wasn't far removed
from sex, that it was like a kind of prelude to going
to bed with someone—and that this was the
possibility you were denying yourself,
so well-versed were you in the art of denial
you never realized you were cashing
in your chips before the game even began,

spreading your cards on the table in the shape of a fan
so that one card partially obscured the one behind it,
as if the other players were supposed to be impressed
by your fucking hand (two pairs, I hate to tell you,
won't get you shit in this world).

It was late in the day for dancing, or anything else,
and there were shouts of "man overboard"
from the boat on the horizon, but it wasn't you
sinking fast or flailing your arms
above the water, while the sharks circled around you,
and the music was just a humming now from the
depths of space, from the eerie corridor
between the moon and the sun and the rest of the planets
had collided with the stars which were shrinking
inside their own mini-universes,
showering sparks and embers out into the receding
hairline of the entire astronomical chart
as much as we're able to understand of whatever's out there
while taking into account all the worlds beyond this one
that no one knows about but which are like shadows
of the world as it exists today, the shadow of the body
of the stranger as he hovers above your bed,
the shadow of the lamp on the desk
looming on the ceiling, like a third hand,
all the gestures of love, warmth and friendship
that mean nothing and everything,
the hands on your waist as you circle the room
and the other hands making shadows
on the bedroom wall, the shadows
of the past looming like a gargoyle
above your head,
mouth twisted out of shape, coarse hair

hanging limp over weather-beaten face,
underpants with small red valentines,
crooked teeth.

Some of these poems first appeared in the following magazines:
The American Poetry Review, BOMB, Boog City, Brooklyn Paramount, The Cafe Review, Caliphabet, The Denver Quarterly, Downtown Brooklyn, ETZ, Fell Swoop, Gerry Mulligan, Intervalles, Make (Chicago), *Mimeo Mimeo, Octopus, Pequod, Poems by Sunday, Posit, The Recluse, Staging Ground, Vanitas, X-nay Reader, Zen Monster, 1111.*

★

"Disaster Relief" was published as a broadside by Farfalla Books.
"Durango" was published as a broadside by The Center for Book Arts (New York).
"Donatello" was published in a limited edition by Third Floor Apartment Press.
"New Year's Eve" was published as a broadside by Ken "Angel" Davis.
"Poem" ("You can fire") was published as a baseball card by Fact-Simile Press.
"Dear Communard" was published in the anthology *Poems for the Writing* (edited by Valerie Fox and Lynn Levin).

★

Thanks to Daniel Owen, Michael Newton, Sarah Anne Wallen, Kyle Schlesinger, Jed Birmingham, Steve Clay, Daniel Kane, Mushka Kochan, Joel Craig, Wang Ping, Tod Thilleman, Barbara Henning, Anna Moschovakis, and Matvei Yankelevich.

Photograph by Dan Wonderly

Lewis Warsh is the author of over thirty volumes of poetry, fiction and autobiography, including *One Foot Out the Door: Collected Stories* (Spuyten Duyvil, 2014), *A Place in the Sun* (Spuyten Duyvil, 2010) and *Inseparable: Poems 1995-2005* (Granary Books, 2008). He was co-founder, with Bernadette Mayer, of United Artists Magazine and Books. He has received grants from the National Endowment for the Arts, the New York State Council of the Arts, The Poet's Foundation and The Fund for Poetry. *Mimeo Mimeo #7* (2012) was devoted to his poetry, fiction and collages, and to a bibliography of his work as a writer and publisher. He has taught at Naropa University, The Poetry Project, SUNY Albany and Long Island University (Brooklyn) where he was director of the MFA program in creative writing (2007-2013) and where he currently teaches.